W9-BAX-061

WOLFGANG CLEMEN

SHAKESPEARE'S SOLILOQUIES

FOLCROFT LIBRARY EDITIONS / 1972

Limited to 150 Copies

WOLFGANG CLEMEN

SHAKESPEARE'S SOLILOQUIES

The
Presidential Address of the
Modern Humanities Research
Association
1964

CAMBRIDGE UNIVERSITY PRESS

SHAKESPEARE'S SOLILOQUIES

THE first thing that strikes us about Shakespeare's soliloquies,[1] if we compare them with those of any other dramatist, is their extraordinary variety." Looking at Euripides or Seneca, at Corneille or Racine, at Lessing or Schiller we find that each of these dramatists has developed his own specific but limited manner of composing and using a soliloquy. It is therefore possible to speak of the soliloquy typical of Corneille or Schiller. But what is the typical Shakespeare monologue? We cannot answer this question satisfactorily, for Shakespeare's soliloquies include not only Macbeth's 'If it were done' and Othello's 'It is the cause' but also Launce's comic performance of his family-scene with his dog and his shoes, Richard Gloucester's self-introduction, Malvolio's reading and commenting on Olivia's forged letter, Lear's harangues to the elements, the Porter's speech in *Macbeth*, Falstaff's speech on honour and the Bastard's railings on 'Commodity'. All these are typical of Shakespeare, but differ from each other widely in style, method and function. They are all soliloquies, but have little in common, serving different ends and producing different dramatic effects. We do not seem to gain much for our understand-

I

ing by an attempt at classification and definition. For all these labels, such as 'soliloquy of reflection', 'of resolution', 'of passionate outburst', 'of comment' or 'of self-explanation', only partly fit. By these distinctions we grasp their superficial mark rather than their essence. Indeed, these categories apply with some accuracy only to those less remarkable monologues in Shakespeare's plays which are often given to minor characters but would not occur to us as instances of Shakespeare's 'great monologues'. For those which have become famous for their intensity and dramatic force transcend the pattern and the type. Our approach must therefore not be through classification.

For in this field, too, the complexity of Shakespeare's art eschews such systematic treatment. Although these soliloquies contain recurring features and typical conventions it is not to them that their uniqueness is due. The conventions are not more than ingredients out of which Shakespeare builds up something new.

I have used the term convention and must say a few words on this aspect of Shakespeare's soliloquies.[2] For the convention of the monologue with its lack of psychological probability and its artificiality has often been a stumbling block to critics. There have been prejudices about the use of dramatic conventions. The progress of Shakespeare's dramatic art has largely been measured by its advance towards

2

naturalism, towards a realistic presentation of characters and events. The soliloquy in which a character gives vent to his innermost feelings is far removed from being true to life. Long before the development of the naturalistic drama theorists pointed out the improbability of this convention. Dr Johnson's contemporary in Germany, Gottsched, drily remarked that 'clever people do not speak aloud when they are alone'.[3]

Producers have found it hard to give dramaturgic and psychological credibility to Shakespeare's soliloquies. They have tried to overcome the difficulty of a solitary monologue by adding stage business, movement and other effects. Thus the opinion expressed by the *Encyclopaedia Britannica* in its short article on the monologue, that 'it has always been liable to ridicule' may still be shared by many. Although our age has seen the revival of poetic drama and the turning away from naturalism in the theatre, our apologetic attitude about the convention of the soliloquy, which we feel we ought to defend, betrays the fact that we are still secretly in the grips of naturalism.

Moreover, it was found that not only in pre-Shakespearean drama, but also in Shakespeare's plays the monologue serves a number of purposes which have little or nothing to do with 'self-expression'. For the monologue is used as a means of informing the audience, of identifying characters and explaining their double role, of linking scenes and bridging the gap between them, it is used as a device of exposition and narration, as prologue, commentary and chorus. And all this is still further removed from the self-revelation of a character and has provoked manifold criticism.

However, the stress laid on the conventional features in Shakespeare's soliloquies has given undue importance to what is only *one* aspect among others. The total effect of a soliloquy does not depend on the existence of certain conventions. It derives rather from the whole context in which various factors combine to produce a convincing effect. And then, the conventional element will also convince us. For any convention can be used with a greater or smaller degree of appropriateness. Not the convention in itself is a bad thing but only its indiscriminate, its too obtrusive, its 'unmotivated' use. But this 'motivation' need not necessarily be psychological and has little to do with the soliloquy's adjustment to realistic requirements.

Besides, we must remember that the soliloquy in Shakespeare is only one convention among others. The play in itself is a convention, and Shakespeare constantly uses conventions on several levels. The telescoping of time, the selective method of presentation, the bold imagery and the poetic language— all these are virtually 'conventions' which belong to the tacit agreement that exists between playwright

4

and audience. The test is not the rational and psychological analysis to which scholars may submit the soliloquy afterwards, but the test must be the credibility of the soliloquy within its proper framework. We feel that characters such as Shakespeare creates them, endowing them with a peculiar kind of poetic speech and self-expression, must soliloquize at certain moments of tension, heightened awareness or inner conflict. And we feel, too, that poetic drama, such as Shakespeare shapes it—with its rhythmic sequence of movement and halting suspense, of outer and inner drama—must give space to the monologue. The illusion of character will not be broken by the soliloquy if it has been built up beforehand by similar means, among them again some 'conventions'. This, with some modifications, even applies to our present-day stagecraft and dramaturgy, although it was so much easier in the Elizabethan theatre to use conventions. In particular, the protruding Elizabethan platform stage, creating a closer intimacy between audience and actor, was a better basis for the convention of the soliloquy than our modern stage of scenic illusion. This platform stage placing the actor in the middle of the audience indeed called for the 'direct address' which was often identical with the monologue in its early stages.

However, Shakespeare's art is only partly conventional, it consists rather in a continual transition

5

between conventionalism and naturalism.[4] There is no clear line of division between these two modes of dramatic presentation. We do not even find a conscious and consistent use of convention in Elizabethan drama, as T. S. Eliot has pointed out.[5] Shakespeare's is 'a mixed mode' of dramatic art, he blends realistic and conventional elements and so often and so subtly shifts from the one to the other that we do not know where we are. The criterion must therefore not be the amount of conventionalism or of naturalism which we can trace within a monologue, but its total impact. Shakespeare avails himself both of realism and of conventionalism, but he also transcends both, creating a new and characteristic mode of presentation by which the poetic drama of the Elizabethans became Shakespearean drama. Far from discarding the conventions which he found in the drama before him, Shakespeare exploited the possibilities yielded by these conventions to an even greater extent than his contemporaries. This applies in particular to the soliloquy. Shakespeare constantly discovers new possibilities inherent in the soliloquy, he reveals an extraordinary ingenuity in finding new ways of integrating the soliloquy into the play's organism, adjusting it to the speaker and to the situation as well as to the atmosphere, theme and movement of the play, linking it up with important developments and charging it with dramatic significance and effect.

6

This, then, should be our approach: to ask what Shakespeare can do with a soliloquy and what the soliloquy can do for his play, how he turns the soliloquy into a necessary part of the dramatic structure.

Irritation at the 'unnaturalness' or the 'primitive technique' of the convention of the soliloquy has indeed obscured our recognition of its great positive values. Shakespeare teaches us with his soliloquies not only that a convention—once it has been accepted—can carry conviction if dramatically handled, but also that it can release effects and reveal levels of existence and of inner development which could not otherwise and certainly not by a naturalistic technique be shown to us. I should like to quote two sentences from Una Ellis Fermor's *The Frontiers of Drama*: 'But at its finest, as at the height of the Elizabethan period, the soliloquy, by its rapid and profound revelation of thought and passion, serves the very ends of drama. It reveals what we could not otherwise divine of the depths of the speaker's mind, compressing into some twenty lines of vivid illumination what might else have taken the better part of an act to convey.'[6]

As the phrasing of this passage implies, this perfection of the soliloquy is to be found only at the height of the whole period, that is to say in Shakespeare's great tragedies. But even there we find some instances of soliloquies which—far from being

7

revelations of inner states of mind—are a mere means of informing the audience. Shakespeare's development, on this sector too, is not a consistent one. Throughout his work we find between his monologues great differences regarding the degree of dramatization, of complexity, of integration. With these modifications in mind we may trace various stages in Shakespeare's art of the soliloquy, even within the limited range of a small and necessarily arbitrary selection of about a dozen monologues which I have chosen from more than two hundred.

Richard Gloucester's self-introduction at the beginning of *Richard III* is an example of a soliloquy that serves as an exposition and as an opening to the whole play.[7] This soliloquy has not been prepared for and therefore cannot grow out of the dramatic structure. It is difficult to begin a play in this way and Shakespeare has never attempted to do it again. But in spite of the obviousness and informative function of this self-introduction it strongly impresses Richard's personality on us. Shakespeare here combines within relatively few lines several types of the traditional soliloquy which in the drama before him occurred separately: the expository prologue which reviews the situation, the self-introduction and the planning-monologue which discloses the hero's future aim. The soliloquy is thus made to serve several purposes at a time, a tendency

8

which we can trace in many of Shakespeare's monologues. But the three functions are divided up into three distinct paragraphs. There is no mention of Gloucester's own person during the first thirteen lines beginning:

> Now is the winter of our discontent
> Made glorious summer by this sun of York;

but even these lines, reading like an impersonal epic description rather than a dramatic opening, are tinged by Richard's irony and reveal his spiteful mockery of the warrior's effeminate demeanour who 'instead of mounting barbed steeds' 'capers nimbly in a lady's chamber'.

The following self-portrayal ends with the famous lines

> I am determined to prove a villain
> And hate the idle pleasures of these days.

This crude self-explanation and motivation of his future career as a villain is in keeping with the vice-tradition of the Moralities and has often been quoted as an instance of the primitive expository technique to be found in Shakespeare's early soliloquies. Indeed Richard describes himself as an outside observer, detached and as it were objectively. But even in this passage we seem to hear Richard's own voice when he speaks with scornful awareness of his own deformity, impatiently piling up the phrases:

I—that am curtail'd of this fair proportion,
Cheated of feature by dissembling nature,
Deform'd, unfinish'd, sent before my time
Into this breathing world, scarce half made up.

(18 ff.)

The final announcement of his villainous plans directed against Clarence is an overt 'informing of the audience', though the phrasing betrays Richard's gleeful sarcasm, with which he applauds his own plotting. However, the plan thus laid open before us is a ready-made one, we are not present—as in later soliloquies—while it is hatched. The whole soliloquy is like a well-planned and orderly speech which is given *after* the process of thinking, planning and self-analysis has come to an end; we are told the results but are not drawn into the process itself.

Comparing this soliloquy with possible models in Senecan drama, including its imitations in England, we note how Shakespeare is much more concrete and graphic, integrating many significant details into his soliloquy. Instead of the abstract emotional outbursts or general reflections which we find in Senecan monologues Gloucester's soliloquy contains a wealth of pertinent matter and thus links up with the coming scenes.

The detached attitude in which a character describes himself as if he were an outside observer still applies to the long soliloquy which we hear from Richard II before he is murdered at Pomfret Castle

(v, 5, 1–66). But the self-characterization we find in this soliloquy is more complex and more subtle than in Richard Gloucester's self-introduction and its dramatic function more convincing. After the short conversation between Exton and a Servant (v, 4), which precedes this soliloquy, the audience will expect the murder of the King. This premonition lends a particular tension to Richard's monologue in his prison cell. The loneliness of captivity, the closeness of death, the contrast between a royal past and a miserable present, all this gives a special justification and motivation to Richard's soliloquy. There is no need of exposition or of informing the audience now, so that the soliloquy can concentrate on a full expression of Richard's character and situation. We see Richard here not merely 'explaining' but *doing* something in his soliloquy, though this activity takes place only in his mind. He imagines a little scene that develops out of his initial comparison

> how I may compare
> This prison where I live unto the world.

It is characteristic of the king's imaginative aspiration that this comparison is too far-fetched to be carried out without difficulty:

> I cannot do it. Yet I'll hammer it out.
> My brain I'll prove the female to my soul,
> My soul the father; and these two beget
> A generation of still-breeding thoughts,

And these same thoughts people this little world,
In humours like the people of this world,
For no thought is contented....

These thoughts are then even given a voice and enter
into dialogue with one another: 'Come, little ones'
one group says to the other. The audience, anticipa-
ting the king's impending murder, will follow these
sophisticated speculations with feelings of suspense,
of apprehension and concern. This soliloquy, while
once more arousing our sympathies for the king,
gives us a last portrait of him and epitomizes several
features of his character: his imaginative nature and
his self-deception, his ability to mirror and to pity
himself. It also shows his faculty of not only obser-
ving himself with extraordinary awareness of his
own situation but also of giving poetic expression to
this his own role and state of mind, indulging in
symbolic ceremony and imagery, acting his part
with conscious royal dignity and exploiting the
theatrical possibilities of even his utmost misery.
That this heightened capacity for self-expression
should eventually find its outlet in a long soliloquy
is dramatically convincing. But this self-expression is
by no means spontaneous, it is given with that ex-
plicitness and elaborateness typical of the whole play.
If we hear a statement like

Thus play I in one person many people,
And none contented

we shall accept it as being in keeping with this whole style, although it is a logical deduction and a well-considered self-interpretation rather than an unpremeditated monologic utterance. For even in his soliloquy the king still keeps an eye on the spectators. He *demonstrates* what he is instead of just being what he is by means of his language and his behaviour, leaving the implications to the audience. He is not only his own actor but also his own interpreter and commentator.

But let us not overlook the new features in the handling of this soliloquy: the scene of this soliloquy, the prison, is transformed into a metaphor of inner experience, spoken dialogue (between the various kinds of thoughts) is introduced, the imagination itself is shown at work and the irrevocable and futile passing of time enters the king's inner consciousness by that fine comparison of himself with a 'numb'ring clock'. Indeed the emphasis in this soliloquy is no longer, as in Gloucester's self-introduction, on outward experience, on plans and political circumstances, but on inner experience.

But an introverted self-awareness is only one of the conditions which may lend credibility and inner motivation to a soliloquy. The Bastard in *King John* is an example of the way in which a character of a very different cast of mind may also use the soliloquy with dramatic cogency. When, at the end of the second act (II, 1, 561), he remains alone on the stage

13

to rail on 'Commodity', he is ostensibly set apart from the rest; his isolation, his being so different from the others, his cynical reaction to what has just happened and his sharp observation of the ways of the world, all these find expression in that famous soliloquy. It is a critical comment on what has just happened, as well as a manifestation of the Bastard's own attitude and his odd character. Indeed, this soliloquy, placed as a mirror at the end of that long scene, makes us look at the preceding dispute with critical awareness so that by this retrospective function we gain a somewhat changed outlook. We see what has happened with the Bastard's eyes, without, however, identifying ourselves wholly with his view. For this very soliloquy in which the Bastard attacks 'Commodity, the bias of the world' reveals that this character's strong individuality is itself not quite without a bias. Of the five soliloquies occurring in *King John* the Bastard is given three, which emphasizes the peculiar position he holds in this play. It is through his soliloquies that the Bastard becomes so alive for us, and it is here that he gives us the best instance of the individual vivid speech with which Shakespeare endowed him. We can also note how the soliloquy is gradually becoming 'acted monologue' which in itself contains the indications for gesture, mien and movement as well as a dramatization through spoken dialogue. We may take the following lines from the Bastard's first soliloquy:

Why then I suck my teeth and catechize
My picked man of countries: 'My dear sir,'
Thus leaning on my elbow, I begin,
'I shall beseech you'—that is question now;
And then comes answer like an Absey book:
'O sir,' says answer, 'at your best command,
At your employment: at your service, sir!'

(I, I, 192)

This is one way of dramatizing a soliloquy. But Shakespeare has tried many other methods of dramatization. In the fourth act of *Romeo and Juliet* we find the scene in which Juliet drinks the 'distilled liquor' given her by Friar Laurence (IV, 3). There are thirteen lines of an introductory talk between Juliet, the Nurse and Lady Capulet, but then for the rest of the scene (for forty-five lines) Juliet is left alone and her long soliloquy is an accompanying text for the action, in the course of which she drinks the vial, deposes a dagger at her bedside and eventually throws herself down on her bed. The soliloquy thus creates and interprets the action, but we still find the self-awareness and 'self-dramatization' so characteristic of Shakespeare,[8] for Juliet introduces her performance by the words: 'My dismal scene I needs must act alone.' The lines that follow are an example of the way in which Shakespeare contrives to combine quite different things in a soliloquy, so that the concept of 'self-reflection' or 'introspection' does not suffice. Doubts about the

15

efficacy of the potion, apprehensions of what might happen if she should wake up before Romeo's arrival, a suggestive pictorial anticipation of the

> vault
> To whose foul mouth no healthsome air breathes in,

a grim illusory scene of 'mangled' Tybalt's resurrection, a parting address to Romeo—all this is made vivid and articulate in Juliet's soliloquy. Even the most rhetorical and stylized of all monologues we find in this play—Juliet's apostrophes:

> Gallop apace you fiery-footed steeds
> Towards Phoebus' lodging;...   (III, 2, 1)

lines which give us a fine relish of gorgeous Elizabethan poetry—are closely linked up with the surrounding atmosphere of the night and the concrete situation. The night and Romeo are interchangeable partners to this monologue and the impatience with which Romeo is expected lends it dramatic immediacy.

Shakespeare has been most ingenious in finding imagined partners for his soliloquizing characters. For the monologue, lacking the real partner on the stage, calls for such fictitious partnership. The monologue in Greek and Roman tragedy had developed the apostrophe as a sort of substitute for this lacking partnership. The apostrophe could be addressed either to the speaker himself, to his heart,

16

his thoughts, his eyes and other physical attributes or to an absent person, or to heaven, hell and the elements, or to some personification. Shakespeare, in his soliloquies, links up with almost all of these traditions. But the partnership which he introduces in his soliloquies is—as a rule—more closely tied up with the situation and more concrete than it had been in Senecan drama.

Thus King Henry IV addressing 'sleep, Nature's soft nurse' during a sleepless night in Westminster Palace (2 *King Henry IV*, III, 1, 5–31) forms an unforgettable scene which illustrates for us the tragedy of this King 'so wan with care'. And of equal symbolic import, again expressing a whole and complicated case both through soliloquy *and* scenic representation, is Prince Hal's address to the golden crown, the 'polish'd perturbation! golden care!' which he, still speaking in soliloquy, seizes and carries out of the room in which the king will instantly wake up to find himself bereft of his royal emblem (2 *King Henry IV*, IV, 5). Even addresses to abstract personifications can achieve an immediate dramatic impact when used within the appropriate context. In *Julius Caesar*, in the scene of Brutus' nocturnal conference with the conspirators in his house (II, 1), Brutus is given five short monologues before the party of Cassius, Casca and the others actually enters. The last of these soliloquies consists of a repeated address to 'Conspiracy':

17

<pre>
                              O conspiracy,
          Sham'st thou to show thy dang'rous brow by night,
          When evils are most free?...   (77)
</pre>

But this personification has not only been prepared for by Brutus' preceding meditations, it is,
together with its imagery, born out of the whole
situation, for the conspirators are waiting before the
door and will enter at once, coming out of the dark
night with their faces 'buried in their cloaks' (74).
Of even greater closeness to the concrete situation is
Othello's address in his last soliloquy:

<pre>
          Put out the light, and then put out the light;
                                             (v, 2, 6)
</pre>

for the candle which burns before Desdemona's bed
also stands for the light of Desdemona's life and the
soliloquy thus condenses the essence of this decisive
moment into a symbolic image which could not be
more simple, more cogent, more appropriate.

The most forceful example, however, for the
emergence of a symbolic partner in a soliloquy is
Macbeth's dialogue with the phantom-dagger (II, 1,
33). Here 'the heat-oppressed brain' (39) has
created by the power of imagination its symbolic
counterpart. The dagger is more than a mere
recipient of a speech, it has become a fearful partner
in a process of struggle, hesitation and final resolution which is transposed into this compelling and
terrible picture of the receding, bleeding dagger

which, though not palpable and indeed a 'false creation' (38), is nevertheless more real than any real object could be.

Macbeth appears from the very beginning predestined for monologic speech. His asides during the first encounter with the witches are no longer in the tradition of information for the audience but are called forth as spontaneous utterances prompted by his disposition for sudden absorption which his partner Banquo early observes in him (1, 3, 57; 143). There is an imperceptible transition from these asides to longer asides which are indeed short soliloquies. And when Macbeth in the seventh scene enters for his first long soliloquy, 'If it were done when 'tis done', we have learned to know him as a character from whom we might expect this kind of lonely labouring self-reflection which combines visionary imagination and suffering obsession with a lucid awareness of his criminal purpose. But 'reflection' is no adequate term to cover the depth and range of Macbeth's soliloquies. For these soliloquies not only show us his mind at work, so that we enter into a process of thought and believe ourselves present while these thoughts are being formed, these soliloquies by virtue of Macbeth's imagination also carry the inner drama to a higher plane of metaphysical vision, they expand as it were the whole tragedy's scope so that we get a glimpse of things which may happen in another world. In Macbeth's and Lady Macbeth's soliloquies the powers of evil and the powers of good assume shape, they become realities and appear before our inner eye.

Shakespeare's supreme art of illustrating an inner process, of expressing feelings, thoughts and moods not by abstract terms but by concrete images and precise symbols, has reached its climax in these soliloquies by Macbeth. The dramatization of the soliloquy, too, is particularly forceful here, as we not only watch with eager tension the way in which an inner conflict is made articulate through poetic vision, but we also see a development taking place each time so that the point reached at the end of the soliloquy is different from the attitude at its outset. Macbeth is no longer describing—as if from outside—what passes in himself; we are in fact drawn into the process of his inner experience which fuses thinking, feeling, imaginative vision into one complex mood. When Brutus, during the scene we have just mentioned, says in his fourth short soliloquy

> Between the acting of a dreadful thing
> And the first motion, all the interim is
> Like a phantasma or a hideous dream,
>
> (II, 1, 63)

he still describes and states what in Macbeth's soliloquy has taken the form of a direct expression of something that happens within himself at just this moment.

We would have to go to great lengths to do full justice to Shakespeare's art of the soliloquy as it emerges in *Hamlet*, *Macbeth* and *Lear*. But it is clear that we would miss half the play and fail to understand these characters if we had not their soliloquies. In these soliloquies Shakespeare has not only developed a new mode of character revelation, he has also simultaneously worked out a new form of drama which by putting the emphasis on the inner drama and on a complex dramatic representation which proceeds on several levels calls for the soliloquy as an indispensable and subtle instrument. Each soliloquy comes at a significant moment and it carries on developments and reveals inner moods which can be made articulate in an appropriate manner only through monologic speech. *Such as*

This is not to mean that all soliloquies in these plays consist of revelations of inner experience. Let us look for one moment at Hamlet's first soliloquy after King Claudius, with the Queen and the courtiers, has left the stage. During this scene Hamlet—though appearing for the first time in this play—has *remained silent &* been reticent to speak though our attention has been focused on his person all the time. When he remains alone on the stage we know that he will now open his mouth and speak without the restraint he has forced upon himself in the presence

21

of others. But what we get in his soliloquy 'O that this too too solid flesh would melt' is not a train of thought nor a consistent process of feeling but a turmoil of emotion, recollection, and violent accusation breaking out into disrupted outcries, exclamations and sudden recognitions. The agonizing scene through which he has just passed transforms itself into vivid images and concrete symbols which flash before his mind to express not only his disgust at the world as it now presents itself to him, but also his clear remembrance and his love of his father, and his poignant realization of the 'hasty marriage'. We too, the audience, may live again through this past scene for which the soliloquy gives us the right background so that retrospectively this scene assumes a new significance for us. The soliloquy thus carries the tragedy to a different plane of reality and we are given new eyes, Hamlet's eyes, to look back at what has happened and to guess at what is still hidden in the future. In Hamlet's soliloquies Shakespeare has created a new kind of dramatic speech which by its rapid transitions, its dissolution of syntax, its extraordinary economy and its fusion of several emotions and ideas can follow the quickly changing reactions of a sensitive mind better than speech in dialogue ever could.

But what about 'To be or not to be'? It is a superb example of the way in which Shakespeare turns into monologic speech an intricate chain of

22

thought which is, as it were, connected sub-
terraneously so that only parts of it reach the surface
of the spoken text leaving it to us to supplement the
missing links. But this most celebrated soliloquy,
I venture to say, is one of the less typical of Shakespeare's monologues. For it is one of the very few
soliloquies entirely given to 'reflection'. Shakespeare's soliloquizing characters, as a rule, not only
think but feel and see, they look at themselves and at
others, they remember and anticipate, they have
their visions and presentiments, they address absent
partners, they plan and make up their minds. But
here a man only thinks and though the thought is
transformed into unforgettable images it does not
anywhere link up with the inner or outward action.
And this sheer detached meditation, although most
characteristic of Hamlet's present mood, is indeed
rare in Shakespeare.

In Lear's monologic speeches to an even greater
extent than in Hamlet's Shakespeare has discovered
the freedom given by the soliloquy to express in
concentrated language the medley of images, visions
and thoughts before they have been filtered, adjusted
and arranged in orderly sequence for communicative
speech as it is used in dialogue. This, to be sure, does
not apply to all soliloquies and not even to all
passages in those soliloquies which could here be
quoted for the use of such 'monologic language'.
Shakespeare has not pursued this path to its end, he

23

has given us merely inklings of what might pass through a character's mind if he were endowed with the faculty to speak out when left alone.

It is necessary to recognize these modifications in order to understand the curious mixture of poetic licence, convention and quite unconventional expression which we find in these monologic speeches. For it appears that Shakespeare, exploiting the convention of the soliloquy, has nowhere moved farther away from 'conventional language' than in his soliloquies. Of the monologues spoken by Richard III, Richard II, the Bastard, Henry IV, Romeo and Juliet it could be said that their diction and structure do not differ much from speech as used in Shakespeare's dialogue-scenes in those same plays. In Hamlet's, Lear's, Macbeth's soliloquies, however, something new emerges; their crucial passages are built up and worded in such a manner that they would not fit into dialogic speech.

But, as I said before, this holds true only with modifications. For even in Hamlet's passionate out-bursts we find relics of the old conventions, the announcement of future plans and the explanation of his own behaviour (obviously meant for the audience), features which have little to do with 'monologic self-expression'. The last eighteen lines of Hamlet's long soliloquy spoken after the Hecuba speech of the First Player in which Hamlet puts forth his plan of the mouse-trap play

24

are only one instance of the way these conventions live on. Nor should we forget that *King Lear*, which has some of the most remarkable monologic speeches (spoken by the king himself), also contains some of the most primitive self-explanations in the short monologues spoken by Edgar, Kent and Edmund who declare what they are and why they behave as they do. Shakespeare did not care whether he applied these primitive devices in his soliloquies[9] which, in the same play, he could transform into a medium of extraordinary intensity and boldness. And his late Romances[10] afford many instances of the survival of these primitive techniques in the soliloquies. Shakespeare made use of these conventions wherever he needed them and he would have smiled at our critical distinctions. His greatness lies not in the consistency but in the inconsistency, or let us better say freedom, with which he availed himself of all possible resources of dramatic tradition and stagecraft to create plays the mystery of which we shall not and should not exhaust.

NOTES

1   The most comprehensive treatment of Shakespeare's soliloquies, discussing their various functions, still is M. L. Arnold, *The Soliloquies of Shakespeare. A Study in Technic* (1911).

25

2 For a discussion of the convention of the soliloquy in Shakespearean and Elizabethan drama see among others: H. Granville-Barker, *Prefaces to Shakespeare* (1958), vol. I, pp. 16 f.; M. C. Bradbrook, *Themes and Conventions of Elizabethan Tragedy* (1935), pp. 124 ff.; A. C. Sprague, *Shakespeare and the Audience* (1935), pp. 62 ff.; B. L. Joseph, *Elizabethan Acting* (1951), pp. 117 ff.; Arthur Sewell, *Character and Society in Shakespeare* (1951), p. 22; E. F. C. Ludowyk, *Understanding Shakespeare* (1962), p. 35.

3 'Kluge Leute aber pflegen nicht laut zu reden, wenn sie allein sind', Gottsched, *Versuch einer kritischen Dichtkunst* (4. Auflage, Leipzig, 1751), p. 648.

4 Cf. S. L. Bethell, *Shakespeare and the Popular Dramatic Tradition* (1944), ch. I.

5 T. S. Eliot, *Selected Essays* (1932), p. 115.

6 Una Ellis-Fermor, *The Frontiers of Drama* (1945), p. 105.

7 For a detailed interpretation of this soliloquy see my *Kommentar zu Shakespeares Richard III* (1957).

8 Cf. T. S. Eliot, 'Shakespeare and the Stoicism of Seneca', *Selected Essays* (1932), p. 129.

9 Many instances of Shakespeare's use of primitive devices in his soliloquies are pointed out by L. L. Schücking in *Character Problems in Shakespeare's Plays* (1922).

10 On the 'frankly informative' quality of the soliloquies in *Cymbeline* cf. H. Granville-Barker, *Prefaces to Shakespeare*, Second Series (1946), pp. 240 f.

This presidential address was read for Professor Wolfgang Clemen by Professor Wolfgang B. Fleischmann at the Annual Meeting of the Modern Humanities Research Association in Chicago on 28 December 1963, and delivered by Professor Clemen at the Annual Meeting in London on 3 January 1964. It was printed at the University Printing House, Cambridge (Brooke Crutchley, University Printer), and published in 1964 by the Syndics of the Cambridge University Press on behalf of the Modern Humanities Research Association.